HOW TO BEWITCH

HOW TO BEWITCH

A MANUAL OF MODERN WITCHCRAFT

RAVEN TEMPEST

CASSELL&CO

First published in the United Kingdom in 2001 by Cassell & Co
A Member of the Orion Publishing Group

Text copyright © 2001 Raven Tempest
Design & layout copyright © 2001 Cassell & Co

Distributed in the United States of America by Sterling Publishing Co., Inc.
387 Park Avenue South, New York, NY 10016-8810

A CIP catalogue record for this book is available from the British Library

ISBN 0 304 35623 9 hardback

ISBN 0 304 35799 5 paperback

Designed by Richard Carr
Printed and bound in Slovenia
by DELO tiskarna by arrangement with Korotan

Cassell & Co
Wellington House
125 Strand
London WC2R 0BB
United Kingdom

I dedicate this book to my loving parents;
whose guiding spirits have gifted me with the
power of love and strength. And to my
remarkable sister who is a true symbol of
kindness and loyalty.

Wishing to cast
a powerful spell,
Look into my
wishing well.

CONTENTS

PREFACE

I was born a natural Witch – one whose powers come from within – into a magical family in Persia, and our family traditions, origins and values are deeply rooted in healing and the Craft of magic. An important part of my childhood was spent in the East, where spirituality, healing and practical magic formed a natural part of everyday life. To begin with, my magical abilities were mainly nurtured through the loving guidance of my grandmother, mother and sister, who are all practising healers. It is through their teachings, and my own studies, that I have accumulated my extensive knowledge and experience of both Eastern and Western magic. My work focuses mainly on the art of healing and the potent power of magic to create positive changes in the world.

In this book I hope to teach individuals how to nurture the power to alter their own lives by connecting with a higher wisdom and using it to improve their daily lives through magic.

The first part of the book is devoted to the history and practice of Witchcraft, and the opening chapter covers the roots of Witchcraft and the 'burning times', before moving on to the role of modern Witches and the Craft in the new millennium. I also tackle the grave allegations that have been made against Witches, identifying the inherent differences between Witchcraft and Satanism.

The second chapter is dedicated to the powers of the moon in our lives and the correlation between its different phases and the use of magic, and how our positive energies can be directed by the moon so as to best benefit our minds and bodies.

The spell wheel, the basis for casting powerful spells correctly, is introduced in the third chapter. The important dos and don'ts of magic are emphasized, and I describe an effective method of energizing tools for your own purposes. I also explain the significance of the Gods and Goddesses, especially the different roles of the Celtic deities and their momentous presence in our magical workings.

The second part of the book is comprised of the spells, the majority of which are arranged into three chapters, each focusing on a particular aspect of life and covering a wide range of situations. There are approximately sixty spells in all, dealing with love and personal relationships, wealth, success and happiness, and protection and health. The spells are both practical and potent, and they should appeal to both novices and experienced Witches alike.

Raven Tempest
Avebury, 2001

INTRODUCTION

This book is a power in itself. The potent magical formulas within its pages offer you fulfilment, success and inspiration and will transform your life for the better. It also contains a clear step-by-step guide to the enchanting world of the Craft, to which you will be able to relate without fear.

The combination of my own natural experiences with updated knowledge has allowed me to bring forward the powers of the deities from the Dark Ages into the twenty-first century so that everyone can benefit from them. By tapping into the 'Old Religion', as the worship of the ancient Gods and Goddesses is known, you can ignite a supreme source of energy which may then be utilized for the good of all. This may manifest itself on numerous levels, beginning with the mind and body and extending to the directing of healing energies to all living creatures and to the universe as a whole. By giving new life to the old ways and crystallizing them, the Craft offers a positive spiritual path that teaches you how to take better control of your own destiny and equips you with the power of choice.

We all have dreams and ambitions but, for many people, these remain unfulfilled because hopes and aspirations are rarely translated into action. By learning about the rich pool of magic and the great spiritual rewards of the Craft, you can acquire the power to transform one situation into another, provided that you also apply positive personal dedication. My principal advice to anyone wishing to pursue the path of the Gods and Goddesses is to trust and apply your intuition.

During my researches into the Craft I discovered some brilliantly inspiring books on the subject, but I also stumbled upon a few books that simply misguided the reader by confusing Witchcraft with Satanism, which is not the same thing at all (see Chapter one). So be cautious of any person, whether in history or in the present day, who professes to be a Witch, magician or occultist but who teaches the unethical use and abuse of power. Such people are not Witches but black magicians; inevitably the consequences of their actions will be severe and, according to Witches' law, will return to them threefold or more. One way of ensuring that you are upon the sacred path, and that your information is correct, is to investigate the background of the author or the author's subject as well as relying upon your instinct.

Do not let this deter you, however, because I can assure you that the glistening path of the Goddess is an enlightening and gratifying way to live. The magical journey through this book will offer you knowledge, inner strength and a power for you to use wisely. Since my exploration and embrace of the Craft, my life has been filled with love and enchantment, and I hope to pass on this auspicious gift to you.

Part I
CRYSTALLIZING WITCHCRAFT

Chapter One
WITCHCRAFT ANCIENT AND MODERN

THE ROOTS OF WITCHCRAFT

Since ancient times, Witchcraft, or the 'Old Religion', has been deeply rooted in spiritual worship, the wonders of nature and the mysteries of natural magic. In Neolithic times, for example, the earth mounds made by man symbolized the Goddess and her power, and people worshipped rivers because the flow of water was symbolic of the menstrual flow of the Goddess, just as they honoured the mountains as a representation of her sacred belly and breasts, and as being capable of childbirth.

Many followers of the Craft believe that the 'Divine Mother of All' created the universe from her mind and body. This belief has more or less persisted in that there lies at the heart of Witchcraft a religion that has been shaped mainly by the experiences and culture of women.

Many ancient healers were nurses and midwives who applied their natural skills to heal the sick and help women in childbirth. Other workers of magic were descendants of long lines of Witches who were practised in the old folk customs, and they inherited the family's knowledge, along with recipes for brewing potions and curing illnesses.

Working with the elements and the seasonal changes of the 'Wheel of the Year', Witches would use natural medicine, such as herbs and extracts of plants and trees, for their spells. These spells were mainly for healing and for protecting their homes and livelihoods, and were often directed at their livestock and promoting the growth of healthy crops.

As time progressed, Witches throughout Europe continued to seek out ancient sites – the power spots – in order to pay homage to the sacred spirits. But there were also many Witches, usually the older ones, who tended to be solitary, choosing to practise magic and follow the old ways with discretion.

PERSECUTION AND THE 'BURNING TIMES'

Paganism existed without persecution from other religious sects until the right to freedom of religious belief was firmly eradicated by the growth of the Christian Church. By *c.* AD 500 the Church's fear of Witchcraft had still to reach its peak and it was still legal to practise magic. All that was to change. Although the Church continued to allow its male clerics to practise magic, even in church, the same right was not accorded to female healers. All sacred sites of the Goddesses were burned and destroyed, and Witches had to conceal their true identities for fear of persecution. As a result, the status of a Witch as a wise daughter of the earth, a healer in the community, was taken away, to be replaced by a distorted, malignant image, created by the Church in order to put fear into people's hearts.

Most of the misconceptions about Witchcraft stem from the propaganda which was mainly instigated by the early Christian movement and subsequently fuelled by the Catholic and Protestant factions. The Church initiated a hysteria about Witchcraft which swept through Europe, fuelling a fire that eventually became an inferno.

In its pursuit of power, the male-dominated Church enforced its beliefs against Witchcraft by implementing laws that made it both illegal and an offence punishable by death. As a result of its false allegations that Witches were 'the spawn of the devil' and therefore evil, many people were killed – and 80 per cent of these were women. These allegations not only lacked any basis in fact but were a deliberate attempt to ensure that women, especially female healers, were mistrusted and totally suppressed. This opposition continued until the mid-twentieth century, when all the anti-Witchcraft laws were repealed. By then it was too late; irreparable damage had been done and many people had suffered unspeakable deaths, many by burning. Despite all this, the Pagan movement survived, although the Church, even if it had failed to quash Paganism altogether, had certainly tainted it.

CHALLENGING THE MISCONCEPTIONS

Even as we head into the new millennium, some strange ideas about Witchcraft still exist, some comical, others much more serious.

THE POPULAR IMAGE OF A WITCH

The Witches of fairy-tale and pantomime are usually portrayed as old hags with discoloured skin, hooked noses, pointed chins, rotten teeth and unsightly carbuncles on their faces. Clad in black cloaks and pointed hats, and accompanied by a 'familiar', they are essentially sinister characters. There may be an element of truth in these portrayals: the healers of long ago were often widows or spinsters, living alone with only a cat or some other creature for company, at a time when medicine and dentistry were in their infancy and coloured fabrics were a rarity. Inevitably, fear and unfamiliarity led to the growth of some strange stories about them, in which Witches were credited with eating newt's eyeballs and turning people into frogs.

Present-day Witches, however, bear absolutely no resemblance to these stereotypes. Like most women, we are interested in our appearance, taking care of our bodies and complexions and dressing in fashionable clothes. Our diet is more likely to be vegetarian than newt-oriented – and who needs a broomstick when you can use a car! We do wear ceremonial robes for certain rituals but, like uniforms every-where, these confer a certain authority and confidence, serving to focus the mind on the task in hand.

DISTINGUISHING WITCHCRAFT FROM SATANISM

More serious are the allegations that Witchcraft is connected with Satanism, which are totally untrue. Witchcraft has never had any connections, or even any similarities, with Satanism or Devil-worshipping, and this still holds true today.

❖ Witches do *not* worship Satan/the Devil or any other related figure.

❖ Witches believe in the power and strength of the ancient Gods and Goddesses, and in their abilities to promote and bring about goodness.

❖ Witches believe in channelling positive and healing energies into the universe and also in taking strict measures to neutralize and counteract negative, harmful, dangerous and destructive forces. Hence the need for the pentacle circle of protection (see page 60) when undertaking any magical workings.

❖ The laws of Witchcraft strictly state that a Witch shall not cause harm to anyone – adult, child or animal – and that all life is sacred and must therefore be respected. Witches never use their energies to destroy, kill or harm any living creature, unlike the followers of Satan.

❖ Witches do *not* sacrifice animals whereas Satanists do.

❖ Witches wear the pentacle ☆ with one point at the top, whereas Satanists reverse the pentacle.

Now you have been given the above reassurances, I hope you can venture further into my book secure in the knowledge that the Craft is there to bring you hope and an abundance of goodness.

For too long a shadow of doubt has been cast over Witchcraft. The growth of the Witchcraft culture depends on shaking off the false images brought forward from the distant past. Thankfully we are a long way from the burning times and a milestone has been reached, but drive and positive action is still essential to keep the wheel of fate and fortune turning for the good of all.

THE CRAFT IN THE NEW MILLENNIUM

Despite the changing times, the role of modern Witches has not changed greatly from the practices of our divine mothers. The evolution of knowledge about the cosmos has contributed to the growth of our insight into the magical world of the Craft, while ancient discoveries, such as the use of herbs and other plants for healing purposes, have become increasingly accepted, thereby providing us with more powerful tools for our work.

A Witch has not just one particular role to fulfil but many. These may vary according to the individual, depending, for example, on personal choice and the community in which they live. The overall aim of Witches, however, is to assert our powers to create positive changes in the world. This may take the form of bettering our own environment, the lives of others, and the universe as a whole. Since the potential for creating improvements in the world is so necessary, even the smallest of contributions goes a long way towards making a significant beneficial difference to our surroundings.

If you are gifted as a Witch, you have a responsibility, not only to yourself but also to others, to use your magical powers in a positive and careful way. Some Witches may prefer to work alone while others join together to form covens; either way is acceptable. Like other people, Witches are brought together through the sharing of common goals in life.

Witches have interests in many different fields, such as the arts, politics, the environment, science and technology. The added advantage is that we are able to strive towards our ambitions and work for our causes not only at a practical, everyday level, with our feet firmly on the ground, but also at a higher level, through the art of magic. There are many hard-working Witches who are involved in campaigning for the protection of our environment and the welfare of animals and children.

These campaigns may be on a local, national, or even international scale. At present there are covens involved in the promotion of the guardianship of our planet by partaking in environmental issues. The loss of the countryside in the UK has occurred slowly but surely, and the ever-decreasing forest and woodlands are in danger of disappearing altogether. The same situation applies in other parts of the world, such as Africa and Amazonia, where large tracts of forest are being burned down and destroyed.

Other covens actively campaign for the welfare and protection of animals, trying to encourage people to adopt a more humane and compassionate approach towards them. Some covens focus on the safety and well-being of a particular type of animal. The terrible plight of racing greyhounds is just one example. As a result of the racing and betting industries, the majority of these loyal, elegant dogs suffer a terrible fate in return for their years of devotion, but campaigns in the USA have led to the banning of greyhound racing in many states and no doubt other countries will follow suit. Other areas of activity include campaigns to abolish vivisection and the use of animal fur, as well as for the protection of whales and dolphins, and many other animals. As Witches, we work alongside ordinary folk to help stop the suffering of animals, not just in the UK but all around the world.

Another area of concern is the safeguarding of children's welfare. As children are particularly susceptible to harm and corruption, Witches who are parents or who work as volunteers for welfare organizations teach children and young people how to neutralize danger and protect themselves. Naturally, if they are babies or very young, a protection spell will be placed around them to keep them safe. Witches recognize the importance of creating a brighter path for the future generation – and hope. We ensure that our children develop with sharpened awareness and wisdom. Only by teaching the correct ethics and knowledge can we hope that our children will not be oppressed by prejudice and other people's misconceptions. This applies to other people's cultures as well as their own.

It is important that more people become aware of the true nature of a Witch, which, as you will see, is to bring goodness into the world and certainly not to cause harm. The satisfaction to be derived from directing positive energy into the universe or from transcending healing energies to others is extremely fulfilling – so why not try it?

Chapter Two

THE POWERS OF THE MOON

SINCE ancient times the moon has played a significant role in people's lives. There has always been an air of intrigue and a special affinity with the moon, one of the reasons being that the moon's position is approximately a quarter of a million miles from the earth. It is our plant's satellite, a celestial timepiece.

When you observe the magical sky at night and the mesmerizing starry heavens, and the radiance and illumination of the full moon shimmering as it lights up the darkness, you can appreciate why people have worshipped the moon and the sea of stars for so long. The magic of the moon is sacred not only to Witches but also to many people from various cultures in different parts of the world.

Many wonderful myths and tales have been created about

the symbolic and spiritual significance of the moon, or 'the Lady of the Silver Wheel' as it is affectionately known. Throughout time we have learned to honour and appreciate the various influences of the moon and other mysterious heavenly bodies in our lives.

THE MOON AS A SYMBOL

The moon is a powerful symbol of the Triple Goddess, who represents the spiritual growth of wisdom and the evolution of a woman from innocent maiden to loving mother and thence to wise crone. These stages are also a reflection of the four lunar phases – the dark of the moon (just before the new moon), the waxing moon, the full moon, and the waning moon, which are also mirrored by the female menstrual cycles.

You may begin to empathize with some feminist groups who feel that, in a patriarchal society, men have attempted, through science, to dominate the wonders of the moon, thereby undermining the spiritual significance of the moon as a sacred symbol of the great female force.

To discover the mysteries of the universe, it is necessary to use both spirituality and cosmology, but they should be applied in a balanced way, so one does not hinder the growth of the other. To combine the two paths correctly, so that they complement each other, is like creating a blend of past, present and future discoveries.

Traditional perceptions and beliefs are an important part of our heritage and therefore should be maintained, but this does not necessarily imply the end of the road or for further innovations. Findings about our planet are constantly being updated, but the main forces that monopolize the universe still remain the same.

Just as the moon is the mother of the universe, representing the feminine powers of the cosmos, so the sun is the opposite and represents the masculine forces that surround us – the power of the Gods. Both energies are necessary for maintaining a balanced universe: the Yin and the Yang.

Purely in its own right, the power of the moon and the timing of its phases can either enhance or disrupt our bodily rhythms and our lives. It can affect our natural surroundings, such as the weather and especially water, as well as healing work and other magical workings.

Do you have days when you feel quite fragile and over-sensitive, your heart dictating to you and holding sway over reason and logical thinking? Well, that is the influence of the moon working on your mind and body.

Consulting the moon and an astrological chart is a vital part of spell-casting. Some days and months are more beneficial for casting certain spells than other times. Sometimes it is a good idea to take a break from magical workings, especially during an eclipse, which can influence and affect the outcome of your spell by producing an undesirable result.

However, as you familiarize yourself with the different phases of the moon, you will become more confident in adapting your magical tasks in order to achieve the best possible results.

MAGIC AND THE PHASES OF THE MOON

We will now take a closer look at the lunar cycle to see how we can determine the most appropriate timing for our spells.

● NEW MOON

The dark of the moon, when the moon is invisible or the new moon itself, is the most effective time for casting spells concerning new beginnings and the launch of new projects. It

PHASES OF THE MOON

Dark of
the Moon

Waxing
Moon

Full
Moon

Waning
Moon

is generally a time for taking new paths and making fresh plans established on the basis of past experiences. The influence of the new moon can also boost ambitions and careers, so it is a productive time for sowing the seeds of success.

During the new moon, money spells and work spells stand a better chance of being fulfilled than at other times. It is generally a good time for spending money and speculating with a view towards the future. Those who have experienced problems should take advantage of this valuable time to back hunches and await success.

◑ WAXING MOON

The waxing moon is the period between the new moon and the full moon. This is a special time for accumulating strength and for expansion and growth. It is also appropriate for preparing your magical spells for the most promising time, which is the three days before the moon is full.

The waxing moon aids the accomplishment of any undertakings, whether of a practical or a spiritual nature. It is the time for Witches' quests for empowerment and a period in which to enhance our magical powers and our perception of the other world. In fact the closer we come to the full moon, the stronger and more aspiring are our intuitive powers, which in turn leads to a new level of awareness.

FULL MOON

The full moon is the most fortuitous time, especially when it is approaching the witching hour of midnight. Your inner strengths and magical powers will be at their peak. Casting love spells during the full moon assures enchanting outcomes, so if you yearn for more love in your life, now is the time to transcend your desires into the cosmos.

The full moon is also the most appropriate time to give recognition and to pay tribute to the spirits that guide and protect you. During this period, the extrovert aspects of our character begin to appear to be more prominent and so we are generally more outgoing and receptive towards others. So use this time wisely and crystallize your spells into rewarding experiences.

WANING MOON

This is the period when the moon journeys from full to new moon. Casting spells for removing problems, eliminating trouble and neutralizing adversaries and harm is most effective when the moon is on the wane. Protection spells for yourself, your loved ones, your home and material possessions are also best cast during the waning moon.

It is also a time when our bodies are much more susceptible to cleansing, so if you feel that you have neglected your body, it is a good time to cleanse yourself through the process of detoxification. This can be best achieved through healing and herbal remedies, such as drinking teas that help to purify the system. Dieting and exercise also become easier and the results generally last longer, so if you wish to shed a few pounds, begin during the waning moon.

Chapter Three
WEAVING A SPELL

THE SPELL WHEEL

A spell is a projected wish that is channelled through our energies and transcended into the universe. This is achieved by changing levels of consciousness to create the desired result. The basis of all successful magic is the spell wheel, which is pictured opposite. It shows the stages which are essential for casting a powerful spell.

TRANSFORMING A WISH INTO A SPELL

A wish is the seed of a spell and the expression 'you reap what you sow' definitely applies in this case. It is not enough just to hope or fantasize about your personal desires. To turn dreams into reality, you have to transform your wish into a spell but, even then, you need to ensure a successful outcome by the

THE SPELL WHEEL

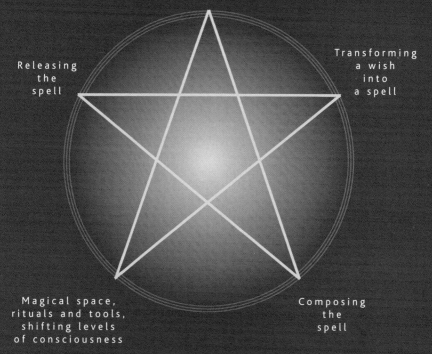

Spell-manifested
thought or wish

Transforming
a wish
into
a spell

Releasing
the
spell

Composing
the
spell

Magical space,
rituals and tools,
shifting levels
of consciousness

actions which you take. For example, if you were to cast a spell to lose weight, it would only work if you took the necessary actions to complement the spell. If you carried on eating too much food, or the wrong type of food, and did not bother to exercise, then the spell would certainly fail. The same principle applies if you were to cast a spell to bring more love into your life. The spell would not work if you just sat at home anticipating the arrival of that love.

The idea is that magical spells work in conjunction with the down-to-earth actions that we need to take in order to create opportunities and open the doors to success. It is up to us to take up the challenge and help ourselves.

COMPOSING THE SPELL

Once you have decided on the spell you wish to cast, the next stage of the spell wheel is to compose it. This is a good way of ensuring that your spell reflects your true wishes and that you have covered all the possible loop-holes. There are two main ways: you can either write down the spell or say it out loud – or you can do both. Writing down a spell has the advantage of giving you the opportunity to change your mind and reword it if you so wish.

An important point to remember is always to ask for your spell to happen in a right way and for it not to cause harm to you or anyone else. By incorporating these words into your spell, you are safeguarding the outcome from any adverse reactions, such as the spell working only as a result of misfortune.

A mistake people sometimes make when casting a spell is to worry about the route their spell should take in order for it to be successful. Please leave the small details to the divine powers, as I can assure you they are the best judges. Remember, the sky is the limit, so do not restrict yourself; the pot of gold at the end of the rainbow is well within your grasp.

Creating spells is great fun and, once you have perfected the art, you can begin to create your own. However, before you do so, please make sure that you have read this whole chapter thoroughly because it is important to know what you are doing, especially when it involves your safety and the safety of others.

DOS AND DON'TS OF MAGIC

DO be careful what you wish for and of the wording of the spell you create and cast. You will get whatever you have asked for, but perhaps not in the way you expected, for example, money as compensation for an accident, or even a death.

DO always ask for the spell to happen in an appropriate way and that it shall not cause harm to you or anyone else.

DO cast all spells within a pentacle circle of protection and while you are in the alpha state.

DO ask for your magic to work for the good of all.

DO take your time with each spell, carefully thinking it through and considering the consequences of your projections.

DO persevere if your magic does not work. It may be that what you asked for may not have been for the good of all. Therefore rethink your spell and try again.

DO make sure that you have taken all practical protective measures before casting a spell of protection. For example, if you are in trouble, you should first contact the appropriate authority (doctor, police, etc.) before casting a spell to reinforce protection.

DON'T ever use magic to cause harm or as a weapon to threaten people. Your action and thoughts will come back to you threefold.

DON'T be flippant when you are casting spells. Think carefully about what you are saying and what you project. Use your intuition as well as your intellect.

DON'T cast spells with children or pets in the same room.

DON'T overdo magic. If you cast too many spells in a month you will burn out your magical energy.

DON'T cast spells during an eclipse because the moon will affect the outcome unfavourably.

DON'T doubt your own magical powers as it will weaken your spell.

DON'T discuss your spells once they are released.

I describe below the essential components of all your spells, whether they are performed in front of your altar or in another chosen place. They should be applied whether you are choosing one of my spells or creating your own.

COMPONENTS OF THE SPELL

Apply the magic formula (see page 59)

Then repeat:

**I appeal to the Divine powers [Gods, Goddesses, or both]
to empower me with their magical skills
and guide me through this spell.**

Say your spell.

**Ask for the spell not to cause you
or anyone else harm.**

So it shall be.

SUMMONING THE GODS AND GODDESSES

To invite the Gods and Goddesses into your magical existence is a way of mirroring their ancient insight and abilities in your life. It is entirely your own choice whether to honour one or both sets of deities. Many Witches tend to follow the Goddess culture because it focuses on female power. It teaches us that the path of the Goddess is the path of every woman, and that we all have the power and ability to enrich our own lives. The Goddess also equips us with the energy and strength to protect ourselves and others. She shows us the path to enlightenment and guides us through our journeys.

However, before deciding on which set of deities is right for you, it is essential that you investigate the subject thoroughly and study the characteristics of the Gods and Goddesses of different cultures, and the myths and legends which surround them. This is an important part of your magical work, so take your time searching for the ones that appeal to you most.

SOME GODS AND GODDESSES FROM
DIFFERENT CULTURES

CELTIC

Bran	Warrior God
Dagda	All-Father
Dian-Cecht	God of Healing
Lugh	Sun God and Master of All Arts
Merlin	God of Magic
Ogma	God of Knowledge
Aine	Moon Goddess
Arianrod	Goddess of Child-Rearing and Motherhood
Astarte	Goddess of Fertility
Brigit	Goddess of Fire, Healing, the Hearth and Home
Cerridwen	Great Mother Goddess
Morgain	Goddess of Witches
Rhiannon	Goddess of the Underworld and Magic
Scathach	Warrior Goddess

GERMAN

Thor	Sky God

GREEK

Zeus	All-Father
Aphrodite	Goddess of the Sky

ICELANDIC

Armathr	Goddess of Prosperity

IRISH

Far Darrig   Fairy God, whose role is to help when
                danger threatens

Nuada   God of the Sky

Blodewedd   Goddess of Enchantment and Beauty

LATVIAN

Majas Kungs God of the Home

LITHUANIA

Saule   Sun Goddess

PERSIAN

Mithra   God of Justice and Light

ROMAN

Jupiter   All-Father and a Sky God

Diana   Goddess of the Hunt, Wilderness and
                Healing, also known as 'Queen of Witches'

Minerva   Goddess of Wisdom

Venus   Goddess of Love

SLAVONIC

Byelobog   God of Good Life and Light; also known as
                the 'White God'

SUMERIAN

Nammu   Mother of the Universe

Ninti   Goddess of Birth

It is an enchanting part of a Witch's life to give valuable recognition to the Gods and Goddesses. By inviting their powerful presence into your life and honouring them, they in turn will envelop you with their love and guidance. I personally invoke and have deep admiration for the Celtic deities, and therefore welcome their awesome presence into my magical rituals, especially my healing work.

To invoke the powers of the mesmerizing Goddesses, such as Brigit the Fire and Hearth Goddess, Aine the Celtic Moon Goddess, Cerridwen the Mother Goddess and Morgain the Goddess of Witches, is to weave the warmth of their passion, knowledge and protection into my life.

Each deity represents a different aspect of ourselves so that, should you be in need of assistance, you can call upon the appropriate deity to help you. For example, if you were having difficulties in love, you would summon a Love Goddess to guide you in finding a solution to your problem.

The deities can also assist you in developing a wealth of understanding about yourself, especially highlighting your talents. For instance, Lugh the Celtic Sun God will show you how to use your strengths to combat your weaknesses. Or should you ever need to have more confidence in yourself, the

Warrior Goddesses will train you in the art of self-empowerment. At the end of the day, however, it is up to each of us to reawaken the powers of the magnificent deities in ourselves because the potential is strikingly evident.

MAGICAL SPACE

Once you have established your spell, you need to prepare yourself and your surroundings. Begin by choosing an area where you can conduct your natural magic. This can be situated anywhere in the house, or even in the garden. A sacred place should be private and away from everyday distractions.

The next step is to create a Witch's altar. This is the place where you can perform your magical work and also keep your special tools and ingredients. This must be your power spot, where you can maximize your energy and fulfil your magical task. You can create as many altars as you wish. Some Witches prefer to have one altar inside the house and one outdoors, in a place of special significance to them.

An altar can be any object, as long as it has room enough for all your tools and ingredients. If you are creatively inclined, you may like to construct the altar yourself. Otherwise, you may like to explore antique shops or secondhand shops for furniture, such as an old wooden chest or a small, inviting table. You do not necessarily need to buy an object; you may already have an item of furniture in the house that you could transform into an altar. Also bear in mind that you may need to perform rituals, such as mixing potions and charging/ energizing tools on your altar. The surface may be made of any type of wood, glass, marble, cork – or even a worktop designed for the kitchen.

The secret of creating a balanced altar is to position it in exactly the right place. This means that it must be facing one of the four main geographical directions: north, east, south or west. Each direction not only serves a different purpose, but also has different powers, which are ruled by various spirit guides. Most cultures have their own unique interpretations of which spirits guide and which elements rule and protect each of the four directions. Therefore, these will vary according to which tradition or school of thought you choose to follow.

Witches keep many personal items on their altars. The only precious item that I would recommend as absolutely necessary is the Witch's pentacle. This is an upright five-pointed star with a circle around it ⊗ and symbolizes the pulsating energy of the universe which surrounds us. Witches use the pentacle for protection against negative and unbalancing energies. It can also neutralize destructive forces and harmful situations, so place a pentacle in the centre of your altar.

Many other tools can be used for protection, such as salt, protection potion and the Egyptian eye (used in the Middle East to ward off bad spirits, as well as for protection and good health), but if you are just starting on your magical journey, the Witch's pentacle will be sufficient for all your needs. There are many captivating and exquisite tools to choose from for your altar but always ensure that there is an item to represent each of the four powerful elements: air, earth, fire, and water. For example:

★ water naturally represents itself, whether in a vase with flowers or in a chalice;

★ candles represent fire;

★ stones and gems represent earth;

★ incense (joss sticks) represents air.

The symbolizing of the elements on your altar will help to establish and maintain the equilibrium of your power spot.

Another important factor to keep in mind is the colour coordination of your altar. Always place the darker coloured objects on the left side and the lighter ones on the right. This especially applies to candles, feathers, gems and any other power objects. The logic behind this theory is that energy enters at the left and is subsequently released from the right. Finally, before you embark on any magical work, it is essential that you keep your pets and children from the room until the spell has been cast.

Once you have organized your altar correctly, you can begin to add your own personal touches. To inspire you, I have listed several of my favourite magical objects below.

★ pentacle
★ crystals/gems
★ candles/candlesticks
★ chalice
★ magical mirror
★ feathers
★ head-dress with gems
★ glistening jewellery
★ wand
★ athame (double-bladed knife)

★ magical calendar

★ pictures of the Goddesses and/or Gods

★ sensuous oils and burner

★ flowers and plants

★ fruits and/or small branches or trees

★ colourful pottery.

Any of the above items can be energized for a magical ritual (see page 58).

Remember, the key to creating a charming, bewitching altar is to listen to your inner voice and apply your imagination. Your altar will become your sanctuary, a haven where you can spend time relaxing and meditating.

RITUALS

As Witches we incorporate rituals into our spiritual work. This is a way of projecting our magical powers through the divine act of a ritual.

Magical rituals are unique and vary according to each Witch and coven. The idea behind spiritual rituals, or their basis, may be the same, but each experience is created to suit the individual. These rituals may be elaborate and time-consuming or they may be quick and simple. Both ways are acceptable and effective methods of projection.

There are certain times during the year, known as 'Sabbats' or 'Witches' festivals', when covens and Witches who practise alone celebrate the elements and the seasons in the form of a unique sacred ritual. This is so we can honour the ever-changing, cyclical patterns of the seasons and the Wheel of Time, which signifies birth, growth, death and decay. Through the concept of shared experiences, which generally take the form of communicating and paying our respects to the Gods and Goddesses and our ancestral spirits, we can learn to gain a perennial insight into the human consciousness and the true value of the Earth.

MAGICAL TOOLS

One of the most highly applied rituals is the art of energizing tools for magical purposes. The idea may sound totally absurd, and you may only have encountered the phenomenon on Star Trek, but I assure you that it is an extremely real and potent act. The idea is to combine your energy with the energy of the

WITCHES' SABBATS

Winter
Solstice
20-23
December

Samhain
31 October

Candlemas
2 February

N

Winter: Earth

Autumn: Water

Spring: Air

W

E

Summer: Fire

S

Autumnal
Equinox
20-23
September

Vernal
Equinox
20-23
March

Lammas
1 August

Beltane
1 May

Summer
Solstice
20-23
June

HOW TO CREATE AND EMPOWER
A MAGICAL TOOL

Before you attempt to do this, make sure that you have thoroughly read the section about shifting consciousness (page 60).

★ Wash your chosen object in sea salt and water. This has the effect of eliminating previous energies.

★ Create a pentacle circle of protection and meditate yourself into alpha level.

★ While holding the object, spend a few minutes observing its temperature.

★ As the temperature rises from cold to hot, begin to squeeze the object.

Then repeat:

I cleanse this object in every way,
it is now ready for me to energize.

★ By squeezing the object, you are energizing it with your powers.

★ When you feel at the height of your power say:

I energize this object [state your purpose]

and then finish it in the same way as other spells:

'So it shall be'.

object through the process of energizing, which consequently releases your wishes into the universe.

Many Witches apply this magical act to empower their amulets for a specific purpose, for example, love, health, wealth and protection.

Sometimes, however, the process of energizing a tool may not be necessary, because certain objects have their own natural magical powers. An example of this is a pink quartz crystal, which naturally attracts loving energies, whether worn by someone or kept in a special place. To energize such a crystal would only enhance its natural powers, thereby creating a mighty tool. The combination of our mental and physical energies interacting with the natural power of an object will always trigger off a magical reaction.

THE MAGIC FORMULA: SPELL-CASTING RITUAL

I will now guide you step by step through the process of shifting levels of consciousness, forming a pentacle circle of protection, and casting and releasing your spell.

① SHIFTING CONSCIOUSNESS

Sit in front of your altar and slowly close your eyes, relaxing your mind and body.

Once you feel sufficiently relaxed, start by counting down from fourteen to one. As you are counting, you may experience a tingling sensation. This is the process of your brainwave activity lowering from the beta state, which is the level our brain is in when we are awake, to the alpha state, which is when we are dreaming and therefore closer to our subconscious. Alpha is the level at which you are able to tap into your psychic powers and project your spells.

② CREATING A PENTACLE CIRCLE OF PROTECTION

Once you have reached this level, you need to create a pentacle circle of protection around your sacred area. The purpose of this circle is to enable you safely to achieve your mental projections with no interferences from negative, unbalancing, inappropriate energies and forces.

To create your circle, you need to imagine that the divine powers which you have chosen for your spell have sent you a ray of silver light. This light is so bright and electrifying that you reach out with both hands and grasp it. The energy of the light will travel down from your fingertips to the palm of your hand and thence to the rest of your body.

Next envisage a bright silver circle forming around you. This circle should include your altar. Then, through your mind's eye (sometimes called the third eye, behind the middle of your forehead), create an imaginary pentacle ☆ at each of the four geographical directions around your altar.

③ PURIFYING THE PENTACLE CIRCLE OF PROTECTION

Now that you have created the safety net around your sacred area, you must invite healing energies to purify your circle. This can be achieved by imagining a second beam of light, which is bright blue. This will fill up the inside of your circle, so that it has the effect of enveloping you. This sea of blue will cleanse your circle and, at the same time, send healing energies into your mind and body. This should make you feel extremely relaxed and secure. Imagine all unsuitable energies being washed away.

Spend as long as you like adjusting to your circle. It should make you feel totally calm and confident in your own strength.

Once you feel ready for the task ahead, take a deep breath and slowly release it. Repeat this a few times.

Next, close your eyes, begin to look through your mind's eye and repeat out loud:

I form this pentacle circle of protection
in the name of the divine powers
[name the chosen deity/deities].

I heal and cleanse my circle, so that it is
free of harmful and incorrect forces.

My circle is now ready and filled with
suitable energies for my magical work.

(4) CASTING YOUR SPELL

Then cast your spell as I have shown you (page 46).

Place all your mental strength and power into the outcome of the spell.

⑤ RELEASING YOUR SPELL

When you have completed your spell, open your pentacle circle of protection by repeating:

> By opening this circle,
>
> I have freed my spell so that it is successful.
>
> So it shall be.

Your spell is like an arrow which you have fired into the universe to land at the right point – and only the sacred powers know where that is. Once your spell has been released, you should prepare yourself to return to the beta level of consciousness.

⑥ RETURNING TO REALITY

Raise your arms into the air with the palms of your hands open. Imagine the silver light leaving your body. As it does so, lower your arms and run your hands over your chakra points (the power points of the mind and body) beginning at the top of your head and ending at your feet. Then push your hands away from yourself.

While you are performing this healing act repeat:

I have now given my mind body and soul a safe healing clearance. I am totally healthy and happy.

Finally start counting up from one to fourteen until you reach beta level.

Now that you are 'back on earth', spend a few minutes adjusting.

You have now returned to this world after successfully casting your first spell. It is important to remember, once a spell has been released, never to doubt yourself or the outcome of the spell. To introduce lack of faith in your own ability is to create a rod for your own back and will result in the weakening of your spell.

If you have followed my guidelines, you can be sure that your spells will triumph. The knowledge that you have accumulated, combined with the gift of faith and positivity, should give you a powerful boost. However, such a gift should be use wisely and with discretion for every good action is followed by a good reaction.

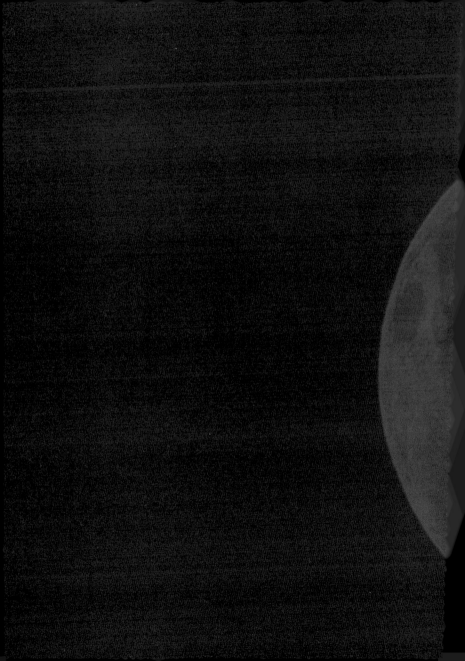

Part II
CASTING YOUR SPELLS

Chapter Four
SUMMONING THE DEITIES

These two spells are to invoke the Goddesses and Gods
in order to express your love and honour them.

HONOURING THE GODDESSES

ESSENTIAL INGREDIENTS

½ loaf of bread
3 apples
bunch of grapes
large white bowl
pinch of cinnamon powder
white candle

Magic formula ♥

- On the day of the full moon, purchase the food.

- Begin by tearing the bread into small pieces and placing them in the bowl.

- Next cut the apples and grapes into small segments and place them in the bowl with the bread.

- Mix thoroughly and add the cinnamon powder.

- Cast the pentacle circle of protection and light the candle in honour of the Goddesses, repeating out loud:

  I honour you magnificent Goddesses.

  I am your daughter and walk in your path.

  I love you and thank you for all you have done for me.

  Please continue your precious presence in my life.

  I offer you this small token, as a recognition and
    appreciation of your love and guidance.

  Please accept my offering.

- Then open the circle of protection, leave the candle to extinguish safely.

- Take the bowl to a park or field where there are crows or ravens.

- Scatter the food and walk away.

HONOURING THE GODS

ESSENTIAL INGREDIENTS

white robe
bottle of red wine
pewter tankard
hematite stone
gold heart pendant

MAGIC FORMULA ♥

- Wearing the white robe, go to the nearest river or sea.

- Pour the wine into the tankard and cast the pentacle circle of protection.

- Raise the tankard towards the sky, and then to the river or sea, and repeat:

    I love and honour you, mighty Gods.

Then pour some wine onto the sand of the shore and repeat:

    I give you this offering as a symbol of my respect and thanks.

    Your important presence is a part of my existence.

- Then take a sip of the wine, pouring the rest into the river or sea, followed by the hematite and the gold pendant.

- Open the pentacle circle and walk away.

summoning the deities

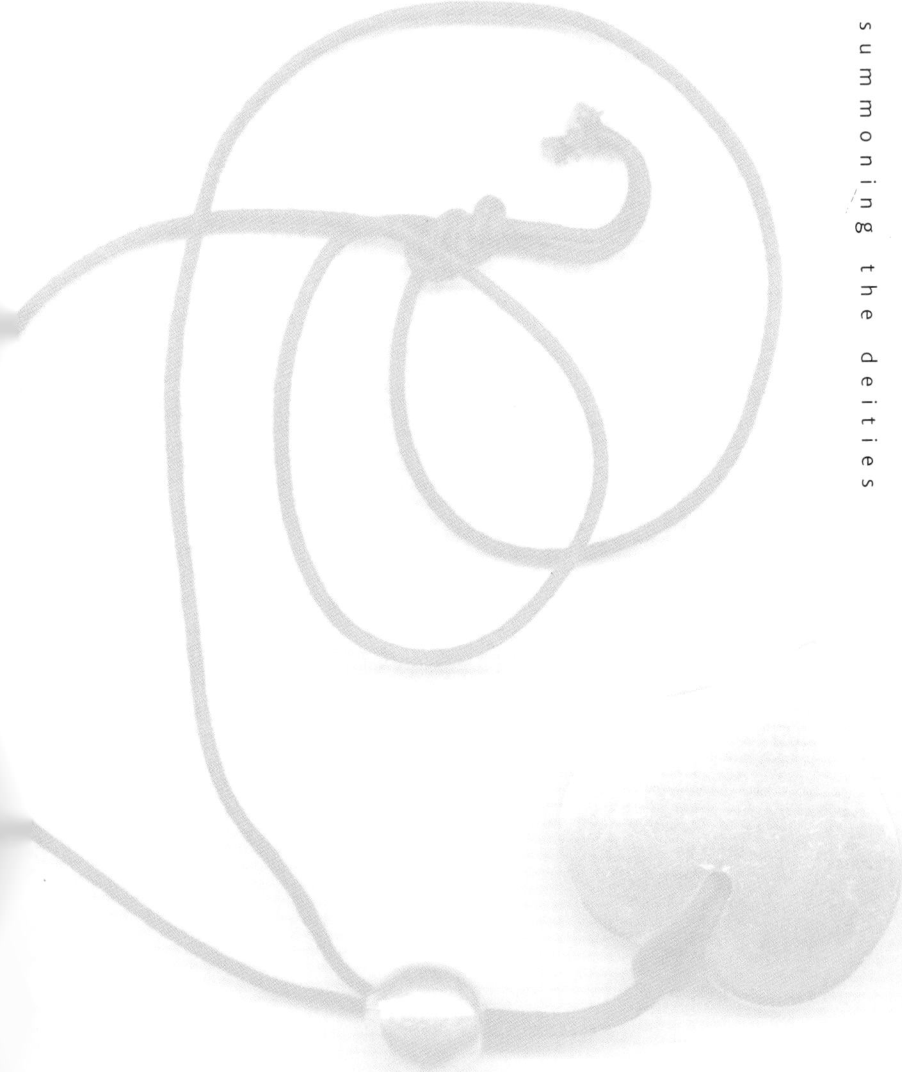

Chapter Five
LOVE SPELLS:
FOR LOVE, SEX AND
PERSONAL RELATIONSHIPS

NINE OF HEARTS
LOVE SPELL

This is a simple spell to fulfil the heart's wishes.

ESSENTIAL INGREDIENTS

sheet of gold paper
nine of hearts (from a normal pack of cards)
black pen
box of matches
enamel bowl

MAGIC FORMULA ♥

- Cast a pentacle circle of protection, write your wish on the gold paper and wrap it around the nine of hearts.

- Burn both items, leaving the ashes in the enamel bowl until your wish is fulfilled.

APPLE-STAR TALISMAN

This is a spell for creating a magical present for someone special in your life.

ESSENTIAL INGREDIENTS

lump of clay
red paint
varnish
5 apple seeds

MAGIC FORMULA ♥

- When the moon is waxing, mould the clay into the shape of an apple.

- Energize the apple seeds with loving, harmonious energies.

- Before the clay sets, cut the apple in half and place all the seeds, in the shape of a star, into one half of the apple.

- Mould the two halves of the apple together.

- Once the clay has dried, paint and varnish the apple.

It is now ready to be given to someone you love as a gift.

PASSION POTION

This is a powerful love potion which is used for attracting love.

ESSENTIAL INGREDIENTS

small saucepan (used only for passion potion)
wooden spoon
chalice or sacred cup of orangeflower/spring water
6 drops of rosewater
1 teaspoonful cinnamon powder
1 tablespoonful strawberry leaves
attractive corked bottle

MAGIC FORMULA ♥

- Send all adults, children and animals out of the kitchen.

- Place all the ingredients on or around the cooker/stove.
  Once you are ready, cast a silver pentacle circle of protection
  around yourself and the area where you are working.

- Place all the ingredients in the saucepan and, using the
  wooden spoon, stir your potion clockwise.

- Simmer the mixture for approximately seven minutes.

- Inhale the powerful aroma of your potion and then energize
  it by continuously stirring the ingredients.

- Then repeat these words:

  I motion this potion to bring me an ocean of love
    that is suitable for me.

  So it shall be.

- Once the mixture has cooled, place it in the bottle and wear
  the bottle as necessary.

PAPYRUS LOVE SPELL

This spell is for attracting the person whom you desire.

ESSENTIAL INGREDIENTS

1 tablespoonful raspberry leaves
1 tablespoonful basil
1 tablespoonful orris root
2 tablespoonsful rosewater
small bowl
piece of papyrus paper
red pen
square piece of red silk

MAGIC FORMULA ♥

- Place the raspberry leaves, basil, orris root and rosewater into the bowl and mix thoroughly.

- While within a silver pentacle circle of protection, write these words on the papyrus paper:

    The one I pine for shall desire me as well, if this is right for both of us.

    So it shall be.

- Place the paper into the mixture in the bowl, cover it with all the love potion ingredients and imagine seeing the person that you desire. Say out loud:

    O Love Goddess [name a specific deity if you wish], bless my spell and sprinkle me with your love magic and help me to be the queen of his love.

- Then take the papyrus paper out of the bowl and place it on the red silk.

- Tie the corners of the red silk together to form a knot. Then carry it with you until you feel that the spell is working.

- This spell can also be adapted so that it is suitable for a man wishing to attract the love of a particular woman.

STAR-CATCHER SPELL

This spell will draw loving energies into your life.

ESSENTIAL INGREDIENTS

thin silver bracelet
pink and red threads
brown feathers (shed naturally by birds in fields or parks)

MAGIC FORMULA ♥

- On the eve of the new moon, wrap the pink and red threads around the bracelet so that they form a five-pointed star with a single point at the top. The bracelet has now been transformed into a pentacle ☆.

- Using either of the coloured threads, attach the feathers to the bottom of the pentacle so that they are hanging down.

- You now have the choice of either energizing the pentacle with loving energies or just hanging it in the window for the Moon Goddess to beam her magic onto it.

CRYSTAL MOON SPELL

This spell is for meeting a suitable partner.

ESSENTIAL INGREDIENTS

silver necklace with a pink quartz crystal embedded in it
few drops of lemon oil

MAGIC FORMULA ❤

- On the night of the full moon, go outside and stand beneath the moon.

- Rub a few drops of lemon oil into the pink quartz crystal and then wear the necklace around your neck.

- Cast your pentacle circle of protection, raise both your hands towards the moon and repeat out loud:

  I invoke the powerful Moon Goddess to cast this spell.
  I wish to met a suitable partner who will enrich my life.

  So it shall be.

- Spend as long as you like experiencing the moon's magic empowering you and your spell.

- When you have finished, wear the necklace until you are satisfied that you have met someone suitable.

HOLLY LOVE SPELL

This is a wonderful spell for winning the heart
of someone you love.

ESSENTIAL INGREDIENTS

small branch of holly
230 mm (9 in) of red ribbon
few drops of love potion (see Passion potion, page 76)

MAGIC FORMULA ♥

- Energize the branch of holly and the red ribbon to help you win the heart of the person you love.

- Imagine your love being reciprocated, resulting in you both being happy.

- While putting a few drops of love potion onto your ribbon, say these words:

  Love and passion light our way,
  Bring me and [name the person you love] together on this
  day.
  But if for some reason it shan't be today,
  Bring us together on another day.

  So it shall be.

- Then wrap the ribbon around the branch and tie it to form three knots.

- Leave the branch on your altar until you notice a favourable change in your relationship.

• Remember, if the spell does not produce the desired outcome straightaway, do not doubt the power of your magic. There is always a reason for delays and you should not be discouraged; all is not lost. It is important not to be distracted by small details at the expense of the main outcome.

RIBBON SPELL

This short spell will bring new love into your life.

Essential ingredients

juniper oil

jasmine oil

30 mm (12 in) each of green, pink and white ribbons

Magic formula ♥

• On the night of the new moon, bathe the ribbons with the oils.

• Energize the ribbons to bring you a new love that will make you happy.

• Place the ribbons together and form one big knot in the middle of them.

• When you have finished and have released your spell, attach the ribbons to an item of your clothing.

LOVE KEY SPELL

This spell is for encouraging someone who is shy
to make the first move.

ESSENTIAL INGREDIENTS

patchouli/strawberry incense
red candle
black candle
key
30 mm (12 in) of red ribbon

MAGIC FORMULA ♥

- On the night of the full moon, just before the witching hour,
  sit in front of your altar.

- Light the incense and candles.

- While meditating on your wish, hold the key in your left
  hand and repeat:

  The key to my heart is jumping,
  So [name the person you want] take the plunge and get my
     heart pumping,
  For my heart is oozing love,
  And I don't want to be losing your love.

  So it shall be.

- Then take the key, hang it on the ribbon and wear it around
  your neck.

- Leave the candles to burn down safely.

CINNAMON SPICE SPELL

This spell will add zest to your love life, especially if you have been stuck in a rut.

ESSENTIAL INGREDIENTS

3 tablespoonsful cinnamon powder
red handkerchief
230 mm (9 in) of red lace

MAGIC FORMULA ♥

- Place the cinnamon powder in the handkerchief and tie it together using the red lace.

- While within a silver pentacle circle of protection, energize the handkerchief and repeat:

   Spicing up my love life, fun in my heart,
      Bring me excitement this spell will start.

   So it shall be.

- Carry the handkerchief in your bag.

- I hope you are ready for this spell because it is very potent.

DELIGHTFUL DINNER SPELL

Perform this ritual if you wish to create a magical dinner
for someone special.

ESSENTIAL INGREDIENTS

gold table cloth
gold and red candles
mixed-leaf salad and dressing
jasmine flowers
passion flowers
olive oil
Italian rice
1 teaspoonful red sage
½ teaspoonful saffron
handful finely chopped coriander
large tomatoes
avocados
wild mushrooms
garlic
red wine

MAGIC FORMULA ♥

- Begin by setting the table and arranging the candles.

- Energize the ingredients with loving energies and happiness.

- Place the mixed-leaf salad into a large bowl and decorate it with the jasmine and passion flowers. You may either buy a pre-prepared salad dressing or create your own, using wine vinegar, olive oil, salt and pepper, walnuts and a dash of French mustard.

- Lightly boil the rice until it is soft, rinse it with cold water and drain. Then empty it into a bowl and add the red sage, saffron and coriander leaves. Mix together with the olive oil and leave on one side.

- Slice the tops off the tomatoes, scoop out the seeds and fill the tomatoes with rice. Then stand them in a greased ovenproof dish and replace the tops. Cook in a moderate oven for 10 to 15 minutes.

- To prepare the mushrooms, lightly grease them with olive oil, add a pinch of coarse salt and a dash of pepper and sprinkle with several grated cloves of garlic. Cook in a moderate oven for 20 minutes and serve hot on a bed of avocados, either as a starter or with the main meal.

- Pour the wine.

I am sure you can think of a dessert!

MAGIC LOVE DOLLS SPELL

This powerful spell will seal the love between
you and your lover.

ESSENTIAL INGREDIENTS

fabric paints
white silk material
white candle
basil
cherry oil
strand of your hair
strand of your lover's hair
330 mm (13 in) each of red and pink ribbons

MAGIC FORMULA ❤

- Begin by painting figures, representing you and your lover, onto the white silk.

- Cut out the figures and create dolls out of them, but be sure to leave enough room to stuff them.

- Within your silver pentacle circle of protection, light the candle and anoint the basil with the cherry oil.

- Once you have done this, fill up the dolls with basil and sew them up.

- Using a small amount of glue, attach the strands of your hair and your lover's hair to the appropriate doll.

- Next write the words 'eternal love' on each ribbon.

- Take the white candle, drip a small amount of wax onto the heart of each doll and place them together so that they are facing each other.

- Finally put the ribbons together, tie one knot in the centre and wrap them around both dolls.

- Ask the Goddess or which ever deity you have chosen to bless your love, then keep your dolls somewhere special.

MAGIC WOOD SPELL

This spell will increase the love between you and your lover.

ESSENTIAL INGREDIENTS

athame

apple

piece of wood (fallen from an oak tree)

pinch of salt

1 tablespoonful vervain

1 tablespoonful yarrow

1 tablespoonful rosemary

MAGIC FORMULA ♥

- This spell can be performed either in the home, if you have an open fireplace, or out in the garden.

- Begin by building a small fire.

- Create a pentacle circle of protection and, using your athame, inscribe your name and your lover's name on the apple. You can also add words such as 'love', 'trust', or 'passion' if you wish.

- Repeat the previous procedure with the oak wood.

- Now you are ready to place all the ingredients, including the wood and the apple, into the fire.

- Spend some time observing the smoke rising from the fire. Notice the different shapes which the flames form.

- When you are ready, say these words:

Mother Goddess, bless this spell, my lover and I shall be
closer day by day.

So it shall be.

- Leave the fire to burn down naturally and safely.

SPEAKING SPELL

This spell is for when you need your partner to contact you.

ESSENTIAL INGREDIENTS

small white candle
photograph of your lover

MAGIC FORMULA ♥

- In a silver pentacle circle of protection, light the candle, hold
the photograph of your lover in your left hand and repeat:

[Your lover's name] to contact me as soon as possible.

So it shall be.

- Then place the photograph on the right-hand side of your
altar.

MARRIAGE-BONDING SPELL

This spell should be performed if you wish to reaffirm your
marriage vows to each other.

ESSENTIAL INGREDIENTS

wedding rings

MAGIC FORMULA ♥

- On the night of the full moon, perform this ritual together.

- Go to a place which holds special memories for both of you.

- One of you must cast a silver pentacle circle of protection
  around both of you.

- Then exchange your wedding rings and, holding them in your
  left hands, clasp your right hands.

- Look into each other's eyes as you both repeat these words:

  Flame of love, O great desire,
  Let my lover's love for me get higher and higher.
  Let us be happy and bond together
  And ensure our love lasts forever.

  So it shall be.

- Then seal the spell with a passionate kiss and return each
  other's rings.

- Release your circle and free your spell.

AMETHYST SPELL

This spell will remind your lover of you.

ESSENTIAL INGREDIENTS

piece of amethyst
framed photograph of you and your lover

MAGIC FORMULA ♥

- Go shopping for a piece of amethyst. It can be any size as long as it catches your eye.

- Take it home and wash it with salt and water.

- While squeezing the amethyst, repeat these words:

    Near or far, I shall be in the good part of your memory,
    Remember me in your heart,
    That we shall never part.

    So it shall be.

- Then place the amethyst in front of the photograph and draw an imaginary silver pentacle circle of protection around the picture and the amethyst.

- Remember always to add that you wish the spell to happen in a good way.

RED HEART SPELL

This spell will help patch up an argument with your lover.

ESSENTIAL INGREDIENTS

9 heart-shaped red floating candles
large glass bowl filled with water

MAGIC FORMULA ♥

- Begin this spell on a Friday night.

- Energize all the candles with loving energies and repeat the following while thinking about your lover:

  Lover be safe, lover be true,
  Lover come back and thrill me through.
  Embrace me in your arms and envelop me in your love.
  Let the fire in our hearts bring back our joyous love.

  So it shall be.

- Spend a few minutes thinking about the words you have said. Then place all the candles into the bowl, light them and repeat the above spell. Imagine you and your lover patching up the argument.

- Leave the candles to burn down naturally.

LIME-LEAF LOVE SPELL

This spell will help your relationship through rough times.

ESSENTIAL INGREDIENTS

2 leaves from a lime tree
honey
pink candle
white candle
black pen

MAGIC FORMULA ♥

- On the day of the full moon, pick a few leaves from a lime tree. Leave them on your altar until the moon is on the wane.

- On the Friday after the full moon, sit in front of your altar and create a silver pentacle circle of protection.

- Light both candles and, using the black pen, write the name of your lover on one leaf and your name on the other. Then, underneath both names, write the words 'reunion' and 'happiness'.

- Pour a drop of honey on one leaf and place the other leaf on top, so that they are pressed together.

- Repeat out loud:

  I neutralize the trouble between my lover and I,
  So that we can be reunited and happy together.

  So it shall be.

- Then place the leaves under your mattress.

ROMANCE SPELL

This spell is for putting the romance back
into your relationship.

ESSENTIAL INGREDIENTS

2 half-coconut shells
4 peach stones
2 whole nutmegs
wild cherry bark
2 tablepoonsful powdered ginseng root
2 tablepoonsful lemon thyme
6 drops musk rose oil

MAGIC FORMULA ♥

- On the night of the new moon, halve all the ingredients and place them into the coconut shells.

- Using your fingertips, mix all the ingredients together in each shell, energize them with romantic energies and repeat:

  I awaken the love and romance between [say your partner's name] and me.

  So it shall be.

- Once you have released the energy, place the coconut shells in your bedroom, ideally near your bed.

LOVE TRIANGLE SPELL

This spell will neutralize the destructive influence of a third
party who is causing trouble in your relationship.

ESSENTIAL INGREDIENTS

sheet of plain white paper
black pen
length of black thread
lily

MAGIC FORMULA ♥

- Travel to the nearest beach, or even a river.

- Standing within your pentacle circle of protection, write the
  following words on the paper:

  I invoke the great Scathach to bless me with magical powers.
  I cast a spell to counteract the power of [name the third party]
  so that she/he cannot cause me or my relationship any harm.

  So it shall be.

- Make sure that you do not wish for any harm to befall the
  third party because the spell will not only be ruined but will
  also come back to you threefold.

- Wrap the spell around the lily and secure it with the black
  thread.

- Try to focus on the harmony between you and your lover.

- Finally open the circle and throw the spell into the water.
  Make sure that it is washed out to sea.

SAND AND SEA SPELL

This spell will empower you with the energy to stand up for yourself against a dominant partner.

ESSENTIAL INGREDIENTS

sea water

sand

stone

purple robe

MAGIC FORMULA ❤

- Go to the seaside and find a quiet spot on the beach where you will not be disturbed.

- Look for a special stone near the water. Once you have found one, wash it in the sea.

- Wearing the robe and, while holding the stone in your left hand, raise both your arms into the air so that they are pointing at the sky. Then stand with your legs slightly apart and take a deep breath,

- Cast a silver pentacle circle of protection around yourself and again raise both your arms towards the sky. Repeat:

    I summon the Great Goddess and the power of the mighty
        sea to bless my magic.
    I cast a spell to energize this stone to give me the power
        and strength to defend and protect myself.

    So it shall be.

- Then, as you squeeze the stone, visualize yourself becoming mentally and physically stronger.
- Next, kneel down in the sand, dab a bit of sand onto your right finger and draw a pentacle over your mind's eye.
- Release the spell and carry the stone with you.

LUCKY EGG SPELL

This spell will neutralize the jealous eye.

ESSENTIAL INGREDIENTS

1 egg
black pen

MAGIC FORMULA ♥

- While standing in front of the kitchen sink, write the name of the person who is jealous of you on the shell of the egg.
- Energize the egg to neutralize the power of that particular person, so that he/she cannot cause you any harm.
- Smash the egg in the sink.
- You will have no more problems from that person.

ANGER-RELEASE SPELL

This is a spell for releasing anger in an appropriate way.

ESSENTIAL INGREDIENTS

purple balloon
black pen
pin

MAGIC FORMULA ♥

- Go and stand at the top of a hill, preferably on a windy day.

- Blow up the balloon and write on it the name of the person who has angered you.

- Then repeat:

    I release my anger correctly.

    So it shall be.

- Pop the balloon, using the pin, and scream at the top of your voice. Imagine all your destructive energies leaving your system and you feeling totally satisfied.

PROTECTION SPELL

This is a powerful spell to cast should you need to protect yourself from someone.

ESSENTIAL INGREDIENTS

black crow's feather
patchouli oil

MAGIC FORMULA ♥

- Create a pentacle circle of protection and burn the patchouli oil.

- Hold the feather in your left hand and repeat the following out loud:

> Warrior Goddess, spirit of might,
>> Bless me with your power and magical sight.
> I now energize this feather to protect me from the threats
>> of harm and actual harm.
> I ask for this protection to come about in a safe and correct
>> way.
> So it shall be.

- When you have completed the ritual, either wear the feather in your hair or carry it with you at all times.

COPING SPELL

This spell will ease the heartache of breaking up
with your lover.

ESSENTIAL INGREDIENTS

2 pink candles
3 drops marjoram oil
pink draw-string pouch
7 violet leaves
2 drops cedarwood oil
2 drops tagette oil (obtainable from select herbal shops)
pinch sea salt

MAGIC FORMULA ♥

- On a Wednesday when the moon is waning, cast a pentacle circle of protection.

- Anoint the candles with marjoram oil and light them.

- Fill the pouch with the violet leaves and pour in the rest of the ingredients. Using your fingertips, mix the leaves together and rub the oil into them.

- Hold the pouch in your left hand and repeat the following several times:

   Awesome Brigit, Goddess of the Heart, give me your
      strength to heal my heart.

   I energize the pouch to heal my pain, I am now happy and
      balanced again.

   So it shall be.

- Then, using the sun finger (the third finger) of your right hand, dab a drop of the oil from the pouch onto your heart and over your mind's eye.

- Close the pouch and leave the candles to burn down.

- Release the spell and carry the pouch close to you.

Chapter Six

GOOD FORTUNE SPELLS: FOR WEALTH, SUCCESS AND HAPPINESS

GENEROUS MAGICAL GIFT

This ritual is for creating a gift of fortune for someone special.

ESSENTIAL INGREDIENTS

pink box
silver or shiny green paper
handful of bay leaves
handful of ash leaves
drop of frankincense oil
gold/silver star

MAGIC FORMULA ☆

- Near to the time of the full moon, cast a pentacle circle of protection.

- Line the box with the silver or green paper and fill it with the two types of leaves.

- Pour a drop of oil onto the leaves and mix them together.

- Energize the star with good fortune, especially for the receiver of the gift. Then place it on top of the leaves and close the box.

- This is a wonderful gift for a friend.

COPPER CASH SPELL

This spell is for attracting money and influence.

ESSENTIAL INGREDIENTS

copper bracelet
1 tablespoonful myrrh powder
2 tablespoonsful basil
2 drops frankincense oil
pinch of salt
small purple bag

MAGIC FORMULA ☆

- Cleanse the bracelet and place the rest of the ingredients into the bag.

- Shake the bag well, place the bracelet in the bag and recite the following words:

  I cast a spell for money and influence to come my way,
  I wish to use them in a good way.

  So it shall be.

- Wear the bracelet on your right wrist and either carry the bag or leave it on your desk at work.

PLANT SPELL

This is another spell for drawing money towards you.

ESSENTIAL INGREDIENTS

3 money plants
pink candle
green candle

MAGIC FORMULA ☆

- On a sunny day, go into the garden and place all the money plants so that they form a pyramid.

- Place the pink candle on the right-hand side of the pyramid and the green candle on the left.

- Light the candles and summon one of the Sun Gods of your choice (see page 48).

- Repeat the following words:

  I summon the powerful Sun God [name the deity] to bless my magic and to shine his energy onto me.
  I cast this spell to bring more money and good fortune into my life.

  So it shall be.

- Visualize an abundance of money coming into your life. Feel the heat of the sun running through your body and empowering you.

- Stare into the flames of the candles and observe their movements in the sun.

- When you have released your spell, leave the candles to extinguish themselves. You may remove the money plants and bring them into your home. Look after the plants as you would any other house-plant.

MARBLE SPELL

This spell will bring success in your endeavours.

ESSENTIAL INGREDIENTS

6 blue marbles
6 green marbles
blue-glass bowl
mint leaves

MAGIC FORMULA ☆

- Begin this spell on the day before the full moon.

- Wash all the marbles with salt and water.

- Cast a pentacle circle of protection and energize the marbles and mint leaves to bring you success and happiness.

- Place all the mint leaves in the glass bowl so that they line the inside.

- Put the marbles on top of the mint leaves and leave the bowl on the windowsill until after the full moon.

PROSPERITY SPELL

This simple spell will help you prosper and forge ahead in life.

ESSENTIAL INGREDIENTS

quartz crystal
330 mm (13 in) of blue ribbon

MAGIC FORMULA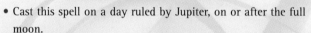

- Cast this spell on a day ruled by Jupiter, on or after the full moon.

- Simply cleanse and energize the crystal to bring you prosperity and improvements in your life.

- Hang the crystal from the ribbon and wear it around your neck for as long as you wish.

MAGICAL SHOES SPELL

A charming spell that will bring you material gains.

ESSENTIAL INGREDIENTS

your favourite shoes
2 gold coins
2 drops patchouli oil

MAGIC FORMULA ☆

- On the night of the new moon, go out into the garden.

- Pour a drop of patchouli oil on each coin.

- Energize the coins to bring you material gain and place one coin in each shoe.

- Put on the shoes, click your heels together and repeat:

  The spell has begun correctly.

  So it shall be.

- Keep the coins in your shoes until the spell has begun to work.

WEALTHY SPELL

This spell will bring you wealth and the finer things in life.

ESSENTIAL INGREDIENTS

gold candle
royal blue candle
handful of mistletoe

MAGIC FORMULA ☆

- Begin this spell at a quarter to twelve on the night of the full moon.

- While in your silver pentacle circle of protection, imagine yourself showered with wealth and good fortune.

- Place the gold candle on the right of your altar and the royal blue candle on the left.

- Light the candles and, while holding the mistletoe, repeat the following:

    Wheel of fortune turn my way,
    I am now rich and wealthy in a correct way.

    So it shall be.

- Leave the mistletoe between the candles on your altar.

URGENT CASH SPELL

This spell is useful if you are in urgent need of cash.

ESSENTIAL INGREDIENTS

white candle
drop of frankincense oil
drop of mint oil
oil burner
pentacle

MAGIC FORMULA ☆

- Prepare a hot bath, using all your favourite oils and cleansers.

- Light the candle and burn both the oils in the burner.

- While relaxing in the bath, imagine all your money problems washing away.

- Place the pentacle over your mind's eye and repeat the following:

  In the name of the Goddess, I cast a spell for my financial situation to improve and for me to have an abundance of cash.

  So it shall be.

- Release the spell and enjoy the rest of your bath.

good fortune spells

RICHES COINS SPELL

This spell will raise your standard of living.

ESSENTIAL INGREDIENTS

necklace with coins (gold or copper) hanging from it
3 copper-coloured candles

MAGIC FORMULA ☆

- On the eve of the new moon, clear the windowsill of any objects and remove the curtains or blinds (to remove the fire hazard).

- Place the candles on the windowsill and weave the necklace around the bottom of all three.

- Light the candles and visualize yourself in better clothes and generally having a better standard of living.

- Then look at the sky and repeat:

  O great power, Lady of the Night, shine great fortune on my life.

  So it shall be.

- Meditate on your spell for a while, then extinguish the candles using your fingers.

- Repeat the spell every night until the candles have burned down.

MONEY MINT SPELL

This is another spell for attracting wealth and good fortune.

ESSENTIAL INGREDIENTS

mortar and pestle
sprinkle of mustard-seed powder
3 tablespoonsful spearmint powder
3 tablespoonsful red clover
3 tablespoonsful star anise

MAGIC FORMULA ☆

- Place all the ingredients in the mortar and pound them well.

- Once the mixture is ready, energize it to bring you wealth and joy.

- Then sprinkle the mixture into your bag/briefcase, or wherever you keep your wallet.

MAGICAL CLAY SPELL

This spell will help you attain the car of your dreams.

ESSENTIAL INGREDIENTS

lump of clay
athame
2 drops peppermint oil
1 drop linseed oil

MAGIC FORMULA ☆

- Mould the clay into the shape of a car.

- Inscribe your name and the words 'dream car' into the clay.

- Once the clay has set and dried, pour the oils onto it and energize it to bring you your dream car, repeating out loud:

    My dream car shall be mine.

    So it shall be.

STEPPING-STONE SPELL

This spell will create opportunities for you to
further your career.

ESSENTIAL INGREDIENTS

large hag-stone (any stone with a hole in it)
small measure of water
silver floating candle

MAGIC FORMULA ☆

- Spend a day at the seaside searching for a large hag-stone
  with at least one prominent hole large enough to hold a
  floating candle.

- When you have discovered one, take it home and rinse the
  sand and all previous energies out of it.

- Pour a small measure of water into the hole in the stone and
  place the candle into it.

- Light the candle and repeat:

  Opportunities shall come my way to better my career.
  I am successful in every way.

  So it shall be.

- Hold the stone and repeat the above several times.

- Meditate on your career prospects improving. When the
  candle has gone out, place the stone in a special place.

WORK SPELL

This spell will ensure that you find and win your desired job.

ESSENTIAL INGREDIENTS

2 green candles
1 copper-coloured candle
cinnamon oil
athame

MAGIC FORMULA ☆

- Using the athame, inscribe your initials and the words 'job', 'success' and 'happiness' on all the candles.

- Anoint the candles with the cinnamon oil and light them. Make sure that the copper candle is between the other two candles.

- Repeat out loud:

   A well-paid job shall be mine, I shall be successful and happy, especially in a financial way.

   So it shall be.

- Visualize yourself having your desired job and being delighted.

LUCKY BOTTLE SPELL

This spell will bring you good luck and success.

ESSENTIAL INGREDIENTS

gold and blue bottle
sandalwood chips
bag of yellow mustard seeds
dried sunflowers
yellow sand
seashells
pinch of salt

MAGIC FORMULA

- Perform this ritual at dawn, before sunrise.

- Cleanse the bottle and fill it to the top with all the ingredients.

- Repeat:

  I create this magic bottle to bring me luck and success in all that I undertake.

  So it shall be.

- Do not put the lid on the bottle. Release the spell and place the bottle in an area where you spend a great deal of time.

INTERVIEW SPELL

This spell is excellent for success in an important interview.

ESSENTIAL INGREDIENTS

gold robe
oak wood
holly
drumming music
spear

MAGIC FORMULA ☆

- The night before your interview, take a cleansing bath and then put on the gold robe.

- Go into the garden and light a fire, using the oak wood and the holly.

- Turn on the music and cast a silver pentacle circle of protection around yourself and the fire.

- Listen to the beat of the drums getting faster and faster.

- Start to let yourself follow the beat of the music. Shake your arms and legs and feel totally free and good. Dance for as long as you wish in order to build up your energy.

- Once you have reached that stage, take the spear and hold it with both hands. Then raise it towards the sky and repeat the following:

  I summon the Goddess of Witches to help me cast this
   spell.

I cast a spell to be successful in my interview and to
  achieve my desired result.

So it shall be.

- Plunge the spear into the fire, then take it out and release the
  spell.

Keep the spear somewhere special.

BUSINESS SPELL

This spell will bring more customers
and better profits from the business.

ESSENTIAL INGREDIENTS

clove oil
turquoise candle
lapis lazuli stone

MAGIC FORMULA ☆

- At the new moon, anoint the candle with the clove oil and
  light it.
- Energize both the candle and the stone to bring more
  customers to your business and better profits.
- Leave the candle to burn down and carry the stone in
  your bag.

good fortune spells

MIGHTY OAK SPELL

This is a basic but potent spell which will rejuvenate you,
either for a specific task or in general.

ESSENTIAL INGREDIENTS

oak tree

MAGIC FORMULA ☆

- Find an oak tree that appeals to you.

- Sit with your back pressed firmly against it.

- Place the palms of your hands on the roots of the tree and
  press down.

- Repeat:

  O mighty oak, magic tree, strengthen me in every way so
  that I can be as strong as you every day.

  So it shall be.

- Stay there for as long as you like.

HAPPINESS POTION

This spell will bring healing and happiness into your life.

ESSENTIAL INGREDIENTS

iron pyrites (fool's gold)
bornite (a mineral, being copper or iron sulphide)
sea salt
water

MAGIC FORMULA ✗

- Perform this ritual on a Thursday when the moon is waxing.

- Wash the pyrites and bornite in sea salt and water

- Leave upoon a windowsill to dry naturally in the sun

- Once dry, energise the mincral and the stone

- Then repeat out loud

    I neutralise and negative energies, forces or thoughts that
    may now be in these

    I charge them to bring happiness, strength and healing into
    my life

    So it shall be

- Once you have completed the process, carry the pyrites and
  bornite on you person for as long as required

WISHING WHEAT SPELL

This ritual is very effective for making your hopes
and dreams come true.

ESSENTIAL INGREDIENTS

500 gm (17fl.oz) of whole wheat
small bowl
small towel
round tray
tea towel

MAGIC FORMULA ☆

- On the day of the new moon, place the wheat in the bowl and cover it with water. Leave it there for three days but change the water daily.

- After the three days, take out the wheat, place it in the small towel and tie it loosely. Leave it for another three days, occasionally spraying it with water.

- On the third day, take out the wheat, sprinkle it onto the tray and cover it with the tea towel. Lightly spray the wheat with water occasionally, so that it stays moist.

- Gradually you will notice that the roots are forming and that the wheat has begun to sprout.

- Remove the tea towel, but continue to spray the wheat with water.

- On the day of the full moon, take the tray to a river and cast a pentacle circle of protection. While tying together a few strands of grass, repeat the following:

I tie these magic knots to bring about the fulfilment
of my wishes.

So it shall be.

- Then remove all the wheat from the tray and throw it into the
river

- Walk away and do not look back because your dream will
come true.

CREATIVITY SPELL

This ritual will inspire you to express your creative qualities.

ESSENTIAL INGREDIENTS

gold paper
purple pen
230 mm (9 in) of gold ribbon

MAGIC FORMULA ☆

- Write the following on the gold paper:

  I summon the wise Ogma to help me activate my creative
  qualities.

  So it shall be.

- Roll up the spell and seal it with the ribbon.

- Place the scroll under your pillow for one night and, in the
morning, burn it.

Chapter Seven

LIFE SPELLS: FOR PROTECTION, SELF-DEVELOPMENT AND GOOD HEALTH

GENERAL PROTECTION SPELL

This simple ritual can be applied to protect yourself,
your family, your animals and home from harm.

ESSENTIAL INGREDIENTS

Mind's eye

MAGIC FORMULA ☆

- Cast a pentacle circle of protection and, using your mind's eye, draw an imaginary blue pentacle ☆ on whomsoever you wish to protect.

- Repeat the following:

  Sacred Brigit, the Triple Goddess, I ask you to protect [name of the person, animal or object] from the threat of, or any kind of, actual harm. I ask you please to ensure that this happens in a correct way. This spell shall not go wrong in any way. This spell is working in an appropriate way and for the good of all.

  I thank you for your help.

  So it shall be.

- Then open the circle and have faith.

- I stress that you should also have taken all practical measures to safeguard whomsoever it is that you are helping.

HOUSE SAFETY SPELL

This spell will help to protect your home.

ESSENTIAL INGREDIENTS

pentacle
lump of turquoise stone
9 bells

MAGIC FORMULA ☆

- Cleanse all the items with salt and water, then energize them with protective energies to guard your house from the threats of harm or actual harm, and for this to be done in a good way.

- Place the pentacle above the front door of your house and the turquoise stone above the back door, and hang the bells from one of the windows.

- Needless to say, you should also take all practical measures to protect your home.

DREAM SPELL

This spell will cleanse your mind of a bad dream that
may have left you feeling anxious.

ESSENTIAL INGREDIENTS

Water

MAGIC FORMULA ☆

- After a bad dream, go to the bathroom sink and run the tap.
- Wash your hands and face in the water and repeat:

    I cleanse my mind and body. I neutralize any negative
    thoughts and feelings. I am refreshed.

    So it shall be.

- You will have erased the after-effect of the bad dream.

BODY-CLEANSING SPELL

This ritual will detoxify your body and leave
you feeling on form.

ESSENTIAL INGREDIENTS

grapefruit bath oil
cypress bath oils
ylang ylang body oil
melissa body oil
geranium body oil

MAGIC FORMULA ☆

- When the moon is on the wane, energize all the ingredients
  to purify and uplift your body. Take a hot bath and pour
  several drops of the grapefruit and cypress oils into the water.

- Visualize all the toxins in your body being washed away and
  feel cleansed.

- Once you have finished your bath, mix together the ylang
  ylang, melissa and geranium body oils and apply them gener-
  ously to your body. As you rub the oils into your skin you
  will feel invigorated and complete.

INCREASING PSYCHIC POWER SPELL

This spell will rejuvenate and increase your psychic abilities.

ESSENTIAL INGREDIENTS

lavender oil
oil burner
ring with a spiral print on it
earthenware bowl
3 tablespoonsful vervain
handful of heather

MAGIC FORMULA ☆

- One hour before the moon is full, cast a pentacle circle of protection and burn the oil.

- Energize your circle with psychic powers and ask the Lady of the Silver Wheel to bless you with a deeper insight into the future.

- Place the ring in the bowl and cover it with the remaining ingredients.

- Leave the bowl overnight and, in the morning, wear the ring on the index finger of your right hand.

REMOVING NEGATIVITY SPELL

This spell will neutralize negative energies and forces.

ESSENTIAL INGREDIENTS

coin

1 tablespoonful black iron powder

MAGIC FORMULA ☆

- In a pentacle circle of protection, hold the coin in your hand and repeat:

  In the name of the Goddess, I cast this spell.
  I energize this coin to banish all negative forces that
    surround me.
  So it shall be.

- Then circle the coin clockwise around your head three times.

- Release the spell and place the coin under your pillow.

- In the morning, bury the coin, sprinkling the black iron powder on top of the coin.

- Cover it over so that it cannot be dug up again because this would break the power of the spell.

RECHARGING PSYCHIC ENERGY SPELL

This spell will boost your energy and recharge
your psychic powers.

ESSENTIAL INGREDIENTS

2 drops jasmine oil
2 drops geranium oil
oil burner
3 clear quartz crystals

MAGIC FORMULA ☆

- Take a soothing bath and pamper yourself.

- Once you have finished, go into the bedroom and burn the oils. Cleanse all the crystals and then lie on your bed.

- Place one crystal over your mind's eye and hold the others, one in each hand. Make sure that the crystal on your forehead is pointing downwards and that the other two crystals are pointing upwards.

- Visualize a mighty surge of gold heat and energy entering through your feet and climbing through your body and into the palms of your hands, where the crystals will light up. This energy will continue rising until it reaches the third crystal, which will light up and release the powers through the top of your head.

- Enjoy all your senses tingling and the pleasure of being revived again.

- Spend as long as you wish lying there, experiencing your mind and body recharging.

- When you have finished the ritual, you will be ready for any magical tasks that you wish to undertake.

POSITIVE INSPIRATION SPELL

This spell will inspire you and reawaken your mind.

ESSENTIAL INGREDIENTS

oyster shell
pink tourmaline
four- or three-leaved clover
small silver magic bag

MAGIC FORMULA ☆

- At twelve o'clock on the night of the full moon, place all the items in the bag and squeeze it.

- Cast the following spell:

   Magic bag, magic bag, filled with positive perception, awaken me so that I can have the benefit of your inspiration.

   So it shall be.

- Release the spell and carry the bag with you.

POSITIVITY POTION

This spell will help you become more positive and will also attract positive energies into your surroundings.

ESSENTIAL INGREDIENTS

3 drops frankincense oil
3 drops juniper oil
3 drops orange oil
3 drops basil oil
large oil burner

MAGIC FORMULA ☆

- Energize the oils to make you more positive and healthy, mentally and physically.

- Pour the oils into the burner and inhale the magical aromas.

- Meditate on the positive aspects in your life.

- You can also perform this ritual at work or anywhere else that you spend a great deal of time.

CONFIDENCE-BOOSTING SPELL

This spell will boost your confidence and encourage
you to love and trust yourself.

ESSENTIAL INGREDIENTS

9 silver candles
large mirror
lavender oil
pink quartz crystal

MAGIC FORMULA ☆

- Arrange the candles to form a circle around yourself and the mirror.

- Burn the lavender oil and cleanse the pink quartz crystal.

- Cast a pentacle circle of protection and light all the candles.

- As you are sitting in front of the mirror, stare at yourself and recite the following:

   I love myself, I trust myself, I have confidence in myself.

- Then energize the crystal and repeat the above eight times.

- When you have completed the spell, wear the crystal close to your heart.

- Leave the candles to burn down safely.

SOLVING A PROBLEM SPELL

This spell will help you to resolve your problems.

ESSENTIAL INGREDIENTS

wood

box of matches

handful of esphand (Persian ingredient obtainable
from Eastern shops)

MAGIC FORMULA ☆

- Go outside and build a fire.

- Sit in front of the fire and think carefully about your problem. Once you have worked out what, or who, is at the root of your trouble, energize the esphand to neutralize the problem.

- Throw it into the fire and watch the sparks fly out of it.

REMOVING ILLNESS SPELL

This spell is for neutralizing ill health.

ESSENTIAL INGREDIENTS

3 cloves of garlic
small amount of salt

MAGIC FORMULA ☆

- In a pentacle circle of protection, energize the cloves of garlic to remove the illness from your body safely.
- Go outdoors, away from your home, and bury the cloves of garlic.
- Place the salt under your mattress and leave it there until you feel healthy again.

GOOD HEALTH SPELL

This spell will bring you good health and good fortune.

ESSENTIAL INGREDIENTS

lemon teabag
brown candle
pink candle

MAGIC FORMULA ☆

- Energize the tea with healthy energies.

- Holding a candle in each hand, repeat:

   Good health and long life blessed with good fortune.

- Then light the candles and repeat;

   I shall always have good health.

   So it shall be.

- Leave the candles to burn and go and make a refreshing cup of lemon tea. As you drink the tea, know that your mind and body are in peak condition.

INDEX